Agnes Ayre's ABCs of Amazing Women

**Newfoundland & Labrador Women of Note
(Some of Whom Won Us the Vote)**

By Jenny Higgins
Illustrated by Jennifer Morgan

BOULDER BOOKS

Library and Archives Canada Cataloguing in Publication

Title: Agnes Ayre's ABCs of amazing women : Newfoundland & Labrador women of note (some of whom won us the vote) / by Jenny Higgins ; illustrated by Jennifer Morgan.

Other titles: ABCs of amazing women

Names: Higgins, Jenny, author. | Morgan, Jennifer, illustrator. | Container of (work): Ayre, Agnes, 1890-1940. Works. Selections.

Identifiers: Canadiana 20190071443 | ISBN 9781999491024 (hardcover)

Subjects: LCSH: Women—Newfoundland and Labrador—Biography. | LCSH: Women—Newfoundland and Labrador—History. | LCSH: Women—Newfoundland and Labrador—Pictorial works. | LCSH: Newfoundland and Labrador—Biography. | LCSH: Newfoundland and Labrador—History. | LCGFT: Biographies.

Classification: LCC HQ1459.N48 H54 2019 | DDC 920.72—dc23

© 2019 Jenny Higgins

Published by Boulder Books
Portugal Cove-St. Philip's, Newfoundland and Labrador
www.boulderbooks.ca

Illustrations, design, and layout: Jennifer Morgan
Editor: Stephanie Porter
Copy editor: Iona Bulgin

Printed in Canada

Excerpts from this publication may be reproduced under licence from Access Copyright, or with the express written permission of Boulder Books Ltd., or as permitted by law. All rights are otherwise reserved and no part of this publications may be reproduced, stored in a retrieval system, or transmitted in any form or by any means, electronic, mechanical, photocopying, scanning, recording, or otherwise, except as specifically authorized.

We acknowledge the financial support of the Government of Newfoundland and Labrador through the Department of Tourism, Culture, Industry and Innovation.

We acknowledge the financial support for our publishing program by the Government of Canada and the Department of Canadian Heritage through the Canada Book Fund.

Introduction

Agnes Ayre here! Welcome to my book of women. I wrote it to honour all of my friends and heroes who accomplished so much in their lifetimes. All of the women you will meet in these pages achieved amazing things—like Ann Harvey, who saved people from a shipwreck, or Georgina Ann Stirling, who became a world-famous opera singer.

But can you imagine what happened when a group of these astounding women decided to work together? They accomplished something truly special. And do you know what else? I was lucky enough to be in that group. You'll learn all about it in a little while, but first I'd like to tell you a bit about myself.

AYRE HERBARIUM, MEMORIAL UNIVERSITY OF NEWFOUNDLAND
NEWFOUNDLAND PLANTS

Wild Cabbage
4 feet tall
Found: Holyrood
September 19, 1927

Aa *Aa*

This drawing is reproduced in:
Ayre, A. M., Wild Flowers of Newfoundland, Part III.
Page 150, no. 479. 1935.

2

Brassica oleracea L.

Holyrood.

September 19th, 1927.

Agnes Ayre

I was born in 1890 in St. John's. When I grew up, I became a botanist. That means I studied plants. I was also an artist. I decided to combine my two passions. I travelled around the island of Newfoundland, collecting flowers and painting pictures of them. I even wrote and illustrated a book, called *Wildflowers of Newfoundland*.

I accomplished a lot, but there was something I couldn't do: I couldn't always vote in elections. That's because I lived before women had the right to vote. I thought it was wrong that I couldn't elect the politicians who created the laws that affected my life. Then I had an idea: maybe I could change the rules! Fortunately, I wasn't alone. A group of other people also wanted women to vote. They were called suffragists. I joined their group and became a suffragist too. We worked together to achieve our grand goal.

Keep reading to find out what happened!

Field Notes:

Memorial University named its plant collection after me:
The Agnes Marion Ayre Herbarium.
The collection includes 2,440 plants that I collected, as well as 1,876 of my drawings and paintings. I am so happy that other scientists and plant lovers can study my work.

Iris, 2 feet tall
Found: Prince's Lookout River
July 1, 1927

Bb *Bb*

Jensen Camp
1916–1921
Tuberculosis hospital founded by Adeline.

The Ladies Avalon Curling Club
Adeline (back row, second from the left) formed the first women's curling club in Newfoundland with her good friend Armine Gosling (standing to the right of Adeline). They also negotiated equal ice privileges for women and men at the rink.

Adeline Browning

My friend Adeline Browning also became a suffragist. You will meet many more suffragists in this book. Like me, Adeline Browning was interested in many different things. One of them was music. She was a talented singer and conductor, and she founded the St. John's Ladies Orchestra in the 1890s. The group played beautiful music and received many standing ovations. Adeline also loved sports. She was a golfer and a curler. In 1905, she helped to create the Ladies Avalon Curling Club.

One of Adeline's greatest passions was medicine. During World War I, she saw that soldiers and sailors were becoming sick with tuberculosis. She decided to help. Adeline arranged for a wounded soldier, Philip Jensen, to tour the island telling his war stories. In 1916, she used the money Philip had raised to open a tuberculosis hospital for military men. It was named Jensen Camp in Philip's honour. It took a lot of determination to raise enough money to open Jensen Camp, but Adeline rose to the challenge. Her great idea and hard work saved a lot of lives.

In 1918, King George V recognized Adeline's remarkable achievement by awarding her the Order of the British Empire. I am so proud of my good friend Adeline Browning!

This is a letter that the suffragists wrote to the government in 1920. You can see my signature and Adeline's here! (Keep reading and you'll meet some of the other women who signed this letter.)

Cc Cc

An underwater earthquake caused the tsunami. The earthquake happened on the Grand Banks at about 5 p.m. on November 18 and triggered an underwater landslide that sent a tsunami racing toward Newfoundland. The giant waves reached the Burin Peninsula at about 7 p.m.

— The worst damage
— Distance Nurse Cherry travelled by horse and by foot

Dorothy Cherry

Dorothy Cherry also saved lives. She was a nurse. In 1929, she left her home in England and moved to Newfoundland. She settled in the town of Lamaline on the Burin Peninsula. Not long after Nurse Cherry arrived, a tsunami struck the Burin Peninsula. On November 18, 1929, three giant ocean waves crashed over the peninsula and swept people's homes and food out to sea. It was almost wintertime, and people were cold and wet without their houses. They got sick. Making matters even worse, the peninsula couldn't contact the outside world for help because its telegraph wires had been damaged! (There were no telephones and computers, so people had to use the telegraph to send messages to each other.)

Nurse Cherry realized that her medical knowledge could save lives. She sprang into action. For six days and nights, she travelled around the peninsula on foot and on horseback treating the ill and the injured. Finally, the rescue ship *Meigle* arrived on November 24 and picked up Nurse Cherry. Dr. H.M. Mosdell, who was on board, was impressed by Nurse Cherry's bravery, hard work, and heroism. This is what he wrote: "It must have been a superhuman effort for Nurse Cherry to make her way on foot all through the stricken area from Lamaline to Lawn, a distance of 20 miles … She was found in a state of collapse after her strenuous and self-sacrificing efforts."

Hooray for the courageous Nurse Cherry!

From the *Evening Telegram* interview with Father Sullivan, November 29, 1929:

> I was aboard the Meigle last Monday when during a blizzard she was brought to the ship in a state of exhaustion. From her we learned a few modest details of her work. From the people themselves we learned of her heroism and of the hardships to which she was exposed. The wave struck Lamaline without warning. For hours Nurse Cherry worked with nothing to protect her feet but a pair of slippers—wading waist deep in water and climbing over wreckage. As soon as the waves had subsided and she was no longer needed on the mainland she gathered a crew to row her to Allan's Island. Two had been injured. She ministered to them and visited the homes of all who asked for attention. When the five communities in and near Lamaline had been cared for her only thought was to obtain a conveyance to take her to distant communities down the coast.

Dorothy Cherry ran the **Newfoundland Outport Nursing and Industrial Association** (NONIA) Centre in Lamaline. She was the first professionally trained nurse stationed on the Burin Peninsula. You'll read more about NONIA and Outport Nursing in "O."

Dd Dd

51 Rennies Mill Road This is where Margaret Duley lived.

Margaret's favourite pastime was driving around the bay, and her trips out of St. John's became research for her books.

Margaret Duley

Margaret Duley was a distinguished writer. In fact, she was the first novelist from Newfoundland and Labrador who had an international audience. Her books were published in London, Toronto, New York, and Sweden. Her readers loved her and so did the critics—she received excellent reviews from *The Times Literary Supplement* and *The New York Times Book Review*. Her four novels are *The Eyes of the Gull* (published in 1936), *Cold Pastoral* (1939), *Highway to Valour* (1941), and *Novelty on Earth* (1942). She also wrote a non-fiction book in 1949 called *The Caribou Hut*. It was about an inn for soldiers that opened in St. John's during World War II.

But long before Margaret started publishing books, she had another goal: to win voting rights for women. That's right—she was part of our growing group of suffragists. She used her talents to write speeches about why women should have the right to vote. As if that's not enough, Margaret was also a talented public speaker and entertainer. When she was a teenager, she travelled to England to study at the London Academy of Music and Dramatic Art.

The well-known British illustrator Gwenda Morgan created these engravings for Margaret's first book, **The Eyes of the Gull**.

Elsie Holloway

Elsie Holloway excelled at photography. Elsie learned how to use the camera from her father, Robert. He was a schoolteacher and a talented photographer who loved to share his interests with his children. Elsie worked hard to develop her skills. When she was 16 years old, she took this photograph of an iceberg near the St. John's harbour. It was such a good photograph that a magazine in England decided to publish it. The magazine was called *Pearson's* and it printed Elsie's photograph in September 1900.

One year later, Elsie travelled to England to study photography. When she finished her studies, she returned to Newfoundland and opened a photography studio in downtown St. John's with her brother, Bert. They named it Holloway Studio. Bert specialized in landscape photography and Elsie specialized in portraits. She especially loved to take photographs of soldiers, children, and Newfoundland dogs.

When World War I broke out, Bert left Newfoundland to fight in Europe. Tragedy struck in 1917, and he was killed in battle. Elsie mourned the loss of her brother, but she also had to keep her photography studio open. She continued to take photographs, and she was very good at it. Soon, everyone wanted Elsie Holloway to take their photograph! She became so popular that she had to hire 12 people to help with all the work. Elsie continued to run Holloway Studio until she retired in 1946. She was 64 years old. What a long and successful career!

Elsie's father took the above photograph of her at a school picnic in 1898. Elsie took the photograph of Kathleen Rorke (below) in the 1920s. At the time, posed photographs were formal and serious, but Elsie's were warm, friendly, and filled with personality.

Elsie took this photograph of Bert in his Newfoundland Regiment uniform.

reply. Surprising to find some otherwise delightful people fly into terrific rages and order us out of their offices, when they learnt what our mission was.

We interviewed all the poli s on both sides—past, present and future. Th d all thought we wanted to overrun the hous sentatives and take away their positions. One day Mrs. McNeil and I and her little dog called on a P.C., now a knight. He did not want to see us or hear us. "I have a headache to-day, ladies, please excuse me. Really I am too tired to see you." He was too polite to have us shown out. "You need some fresh air, my poor man. That's the cure for a headache," said Mrs. McNeil, throwing wide open the office windows. Clouds of dust came flying in, all the papers whirled around and around. We left in a hurry. He afterwards became a staunch supporter, and his wife one of our leaders and a great worker.

We wrote to places all over the island. Wrote again, then once more, to ask if the letter had be received. Wrote to ask what they were doi about it. A f told me she had spent conside able time co the signatures of all the wo her district. One evening in the udy, her rgyman, asked: "What are y seeking, Jane?" "Did Mrs. Smith leave a pack e for me

Ff *Ff*

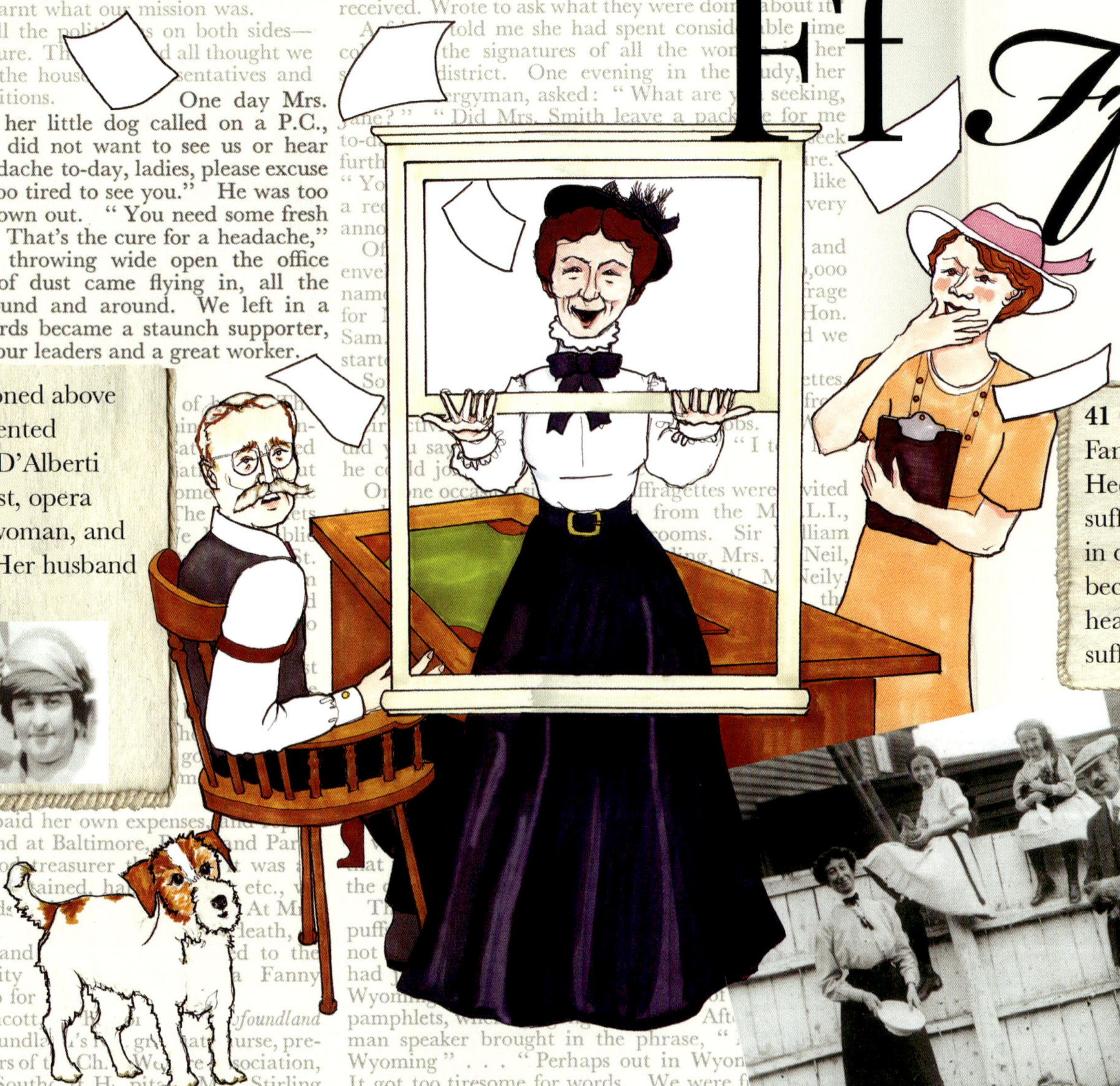

The wife mentioned above was the multitalented Antonia (Tony) D'Alberti Hutton: suffragist, opera singer, businesswoman, and public speaker. Her husband was Charles.

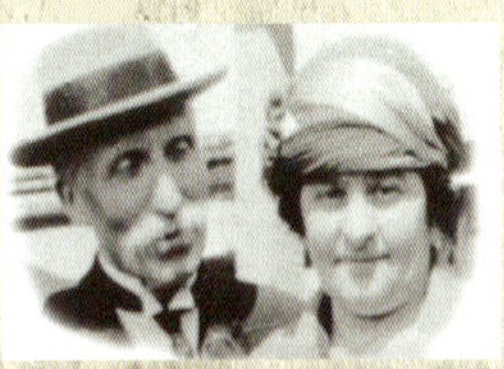

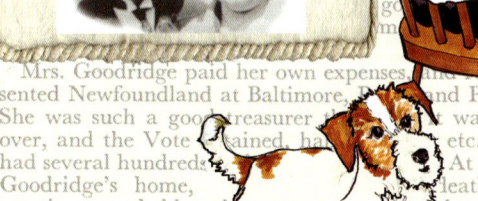

41 Queens Road
Fannie's husband, Hector, was also a suffragist. Their home in downtown St. John's became the unofficial headquarters for the suffrage movement.

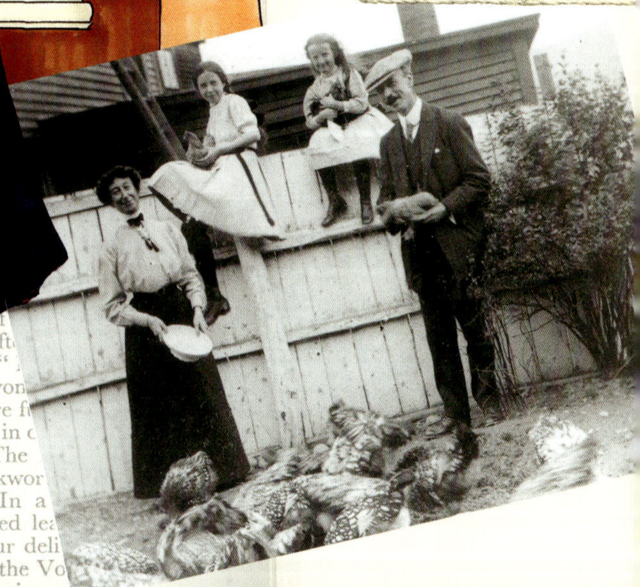

Mrs. Goodridge paid her own expenses, and sented Newfoundland at Baltimore, and Par She was such a good treasurer was over, and the Vote gained, ha etc., had several hundreds At M Goodridge's home, death, meeting was held and d to the Memorial University Fanny McNeil Scholarship for

Miss Mary Southcott, foundland *Wild Flowers*, Newfoundla 's gr urse, president for many years of the Ch. Wo sociation, and owner of the Southc H pita Stirling Fraser, princip f Bishop Spencer College, and her successor Miss Cherrington, Mrs. Archibald Macpherson, Mrs. John Browning, Mrs. Hutton, Mrs. Vincent Burke, Mrs. James Baird Jr., Mrs. Cooper (Southside), Mrs. A. H. Murray, Mr. Charles Hutchings and Miss Crocker, Miss Marguerite Mitchell, Miss Parker and many other well-known Newfoundland women were among the friends and workers.

pamphlets, man speaker brought in the phrase, " Wyoming" . . . "Perhaps out in Wyom It got too tiresome for words. We were f William, gallant man, gave the decision in Soon there was another election. The was being built, a new dock, and Duckwor Hon. Walter Monroe was premier. In a speech, the first act of this distinguished le to introduce the bill himself, and to our deli surprise, the battle was over. We had the Vo A farewell meeting was held in the Casino,

Fannie McNeil

Fannie McNeil was one of the most famous suffragists in all of Newfoundland. She was witty and charming, and she gave really good speeches. Everyone loved to hear her talk. She had fascinating ideas and she told funny jokes. I even worked as her assistant in the suffrage movement. We became great friends. I accompanied her to meetings with politicians and other important people. Not all of the people we spoke with wanted women to have the vote, but that didn't intimidate Fannie!

She wrote about her determination in this article for the *Evening Telegram* in October 1924: "The vote will never be handed to us like sugared cakes, with a 'Help yourself, Madam.' One of our own politicians said, 'Yes, of course you should have the vote—but you'll have to fight for it!' If we really wish to have better conditions, we must help to make them so." Inspiring words, don't you think?

Fannie had other interests too. One of them was art—that's another passion we both shared. In 1925, Fannie and I worked together to create the Newfoundland Society of Art. Fannie even served as one of its first presidents. What a busy and fascinating woman.

This is a letter Fannie wrote to the prime minister of Newfoundland in 1921. She's scolding him because he went back on his promise to introduce a Woman's Suffrage Bill into the House of Assembly. Tsk, tsk, Mr. Prime Minister!

Armine Nutting Gosling

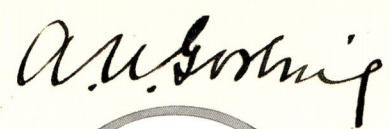

Miss Armine Nutting – Principal 1882-1886.

Armine Gosling was born in Quebec, but she moved to St. John's in 1882 to become principal of the Church of England Girls' School.

Fannie had a good friend named Armine Gosling. She was also a suffragist. In fact, Armine Gosling was one of the group's leaders. We all admired her so much! In 1909, she started a special club where women could meet and talk about politics and other important topics. It was called the Ladies' Reading Room and Current Events Club. (Margaret Duley gave some of her speeches at the Current Events Club.) The club helped us to share ideas and learn from one another. We could also read magazines and newspapers that arrived there from around the world. Soon we became experts on news, politics, and current affairs.

Armine Gosling certainly worked hard for the suffrage movement, but she had many other interests too. One of them was reading. She loved books and she wanted everyone to be able to read. She donated a lot of her family's books to the city of St. John's, and the city used those books to open its first public library. How generous!

Armine also loved sports. She golfed and she was a member of the Avalon Ladies Curling Club, just like her good friend Adeline Browning. (Look back at the photograph of the Avalon Ladies Curling Club on page 4.) Some of the other groups Armine belonged to were the Society for the Protection of Animals, the Child Welfare Association, and the Church of England Orphanage. That's a lot of good causes!

William Gilbert Gosling was a book collector, mayor, and suffragist.

Armine Gosling's daughter (who was named Harriet Armine Gosling) volunteered as a nurse in World War I. She went overseas and drove an ambulance.

Hh Hh

Ann's dog was named Hairy Man. There's another "H" word!

Ann Harvey

Ann Harvey was a fisher and a hero. She had a big brave heart. She was born in 1811 and she lived in Isle aux Morts, a small fishing community on Newfoundland's south coast. On July 12, 1828, Ann was out fishing with her father when she discovered a shipwreck. A large sailing ship called the *Despatch* had crashed into a rock about a mile from land. The *Despatch* was carrying immigrants from Ireland to Quebec. Many people were in danger and Ann had to act fast! She worked with her father, brother, and their Newfoundland dog to pull people to safety. Ann helped to save 163 lives. But it wasn't the end of her adventures. Can you believe that she encountered another shipwreck 10 years later? On September 4, 1838, a Scottish ship called the *Rankin* crashed in almost the exact same spot where the *Despatch* sank. Ann Harvey once again came to the rescue! That time she saved 25 people. Hooray for Ann Harvey: a true hero!

To celebrate Ann's tremendous heroism, the town of Isle aux Morts holds a four-day festival called *Ann Harvey Days* every July. The fun-filled days feature history games, music, dancing, crafts, traditional food, and more!

In 2003, the award-winning author Kevin Major published a book about Ann called *Ann and Seamus*. Three years later, the acclaimed Shallaway choir adapted Major's work into an opera.

In 1987, the Canadian Coast Guard named one of its ships *Ann Harvey* in honour of Ann's heroism.

Ii *Ii*

NEWFOUNDLAND

Our own Newfoundland, swept by tempest and storm
  With thy headlands of grandeur and glory,
We love thee with love and devotion as warm
  As was o'er land belovéd in story.
A brave land art thou, for the storm-king in wrath
  With mountainous billows hath swept thee;
They have thundered and foamed through the ages lo
past,
  But the hand that created hath kept thee.

Isabella wrote the poem "To Miss Twillingate Stirling" for Georgina Ann Stirling, who just happens to be my entry for the letter "N"!

Isabella Whiteford Rogerson

Isabella Whiteford Rogerson was a poet. She was born in Ireland almost 200 years ago, in 1835. Even when she was a little girl, Isabella loved to write and read poetry. She had a big imagination.

When she was 15, Isabella moved to Newfoundland with her parents, three sisters, and two brothers. Can you imagine crossing the Atlantic Ocean in a sailing ship? Isabella's life changed when she moved to St. John's, but one thing remained the same: she continued to write poetry. Some of her poems were about her new life in Newfoundland, and others were about her old home in Ireland. She began to publish some of her poems in local newspapers. Everyone loved Isabella's work so much that she began to write entire books of poetry. Her first volume was published in 1860. It was simply called *Poems*. Her second book came out in 1898 and was called *The Victorian Triumph and Other Poems*.

Isabella was also a very kind and generous person who wanted to help people in need. She saw that there was a lot of poverty in Newfoundland in the 1800s and she wanted to change that. She volunteered for charities that helped to provide education for children and shelter for the homeless. What a big-hearted person Isabella was!

Isabella sometimes signed her poems with the pen name "Caed Mille Failtha," which is Gaelic for "a hundred thousand welcomes."

Jj

Law Society of Newfoundland
The Court House, St. John's.

Louise Saunders was the first woman from Newfoundland to become a lawyer. She was admitted to the bar in 1933 and continued to practice law until her death in 1969, at the age of 72. (Janet was posthumously admitted to the bar in 2016.)

Janet was a great debater—and so were her good friends Fannie McNeil and Tony Hutton. She argued that women should be equal with men under the law.

Janet Miller Ayre Murray

I hope you haven't forgotten the suffragists, because another one is coming right up! This one also happens to be my little sister: the incredible Janet Miller Ayre Murray. Janet was always a trailblazer. She studied law at a time when all the lawyers in Newfoundland were men. In 1913, she became the first woman to be admitted to the Newfoundland Law Society. I was so proud of my little sister.

But her studies were interrupted when World War I broke out in 1914. Janet decided to move to Scotland so that she could be close to her fiancé, Eric. He was serving with the Newfoundland Regiment in Europe. The two were married in Scotland on June 19, 1915. Unfortunately, tragedy struck one year later, when Eric was killed at Beaumont-Hamel on July 1, 1916. We were all so sad. Janet was devastated, but she was also very brave. She knew that too many soldiers were getting injured and she wanted to help. She decided to volunteer as a war nurse. Janet helped many soldiers get better, but she also saw a lot of pain and suffering. I was so relieved when she came home after the war.

You'd think that she'd need a rest after her experiences overseas, but not Janet! She plunged right into the suffrage movement along with me and all the other suffragists. We were lucky to have such a smart, determined, and energetic woman on our side.

Janet and I were both born with the last name Miller, but when we grew up I married Harold Ayre and Janet married his brother Eric (see below). In 1924, Janet got married for a second time, to Andrew Murray.

ᑭ (ki)   ᑯ (ku)   ᑲ (ka)   ᒃ (k)

Kk *Kk*

Labrador women taught traditional skills and literacy. Josephina learned to read and write Inuktitut in Nain. Juliana Boase (left) was the schoolteacher at Okak's Mission School in the early 1900s. You'll meet another teacher in my entry for "R."

Ilinnianik/Education
Felt-tipped pen drawing by Josephina Kalleo.

Josephina's art is now a part of the permanent collection at The Rooms Provincial Art Gallery in St. John's.

Josephina Kalleo

Before Josephina Kalleo became an artist, she raised her five children.

Josephina Kalleo was a talented artist. She was born in Nain, Labrador. When she grew up, she began to draw pictures about her childhood. They show what life was like for her and other Inuit in the 1920s. She drew pictures of people picking berries, walking on snowshoes, playing games, getting married, and going to school. She published 45 of her drawings in a book called *Taipsumane: A Collection of Labrador Stories*. Taipsumane is an Inuktitut word which means "them days." The text in *Taipsumane* was written in two languages: Inuktitut and English.

Josephina worked at the Torng'sok Cultural Centre in Nain. Her job was to listen to recordings of people speaking Inuktitut and then to write down everything they said on paper so that other people could read it. Josephina once said: "I would like for someone to carry on what I've been doing. It would teach the children about what those days were like and they will always know. They should know their traditional way of life." Art is a good way to teach us about the past—and to show us that it's not entirely different from the present!

Ovlosiuktut/Festival Dress
Felt-marker drawing by Josephina Kalleo.

Josephina wrote her book in Inuktitut syllabics. Can you find the syllabic for ka (as in Kalleo) on the previous page?

Lydia and her second husband, Dan Campbell, at their home near Rigolet.

Ll *Ll*

When Lydia was a girl, a snowstorm buried the house where she was staying with an old blind woman. Lydia pushed a high bench to the door to stand on. Then she punched a hole up through the snow so they could breathe. After that she used an axe to cut a tunnel big enough to crawl out. When her father returned, he was so happy to find them both alive. That's one brave 11-year-old!

Lydia Campbell

Lydia Campbell also grew up in Labrador. She was born at Hamilton Inlet in 1818. Her mother, Susan, was an Inuk and her father, Ambrose, was British. They made their living by trapping and hunting in the wintertime and by fishing in the summertime. Every fall, Lydia's family moved from their summer fishing grounds near the coast to their winter hunting grounds further in the bay.

When Lydia grew up, she began to write about her life. She wrote about her childhood memories and also about her experiences as an adult. She published her autobiography in the *Evening Herald* newspaper. It was divided into 13 parts—the first one was printed on December 3, 1894, and the last one appeared on May 17, 1895. Lydia called her autobiography *Sketches of Labrador Life*.

I think this is a beautiful excerpt from Lydia's *Sketches* (it appeared in the *Evening Herald* on December 7, 1894): "I was out the other day walking in the woods with my snow shoes on all alone, looking up at the pretty trees, at the high spruce and birches looking so high and stately. I saw in the sun shine such a pretty sight high above the highest trees, a flock of the beautiful white partridge." How clearly I can picture it! Doesn't it make you want to go outside and enjoy nature?

Map of Labrador

In 2009, the Canadian government paid tribute to Lydia Campbell by making her a Person of National Historic Significance. The government only gives this title to people who have made important contributions to society.

Lydia wasn't the only author in her family. Her great-granddaughter was a writer too. Her name was Elizabeth Goudie, and her book was called *Woman of Labrador*. That's one talented family!

Mm

1 Devon Row
This is where the Women's Franchise League first met in January 1920.

In June, we composed this letter to Newfoundland's prime minister. Can you read the handwriting?

Anna Barnes Mitchell

Marvellous Anna Barnes Mitchell! How much I admire your mettle! Anna was another leader of the suffrage movement. In 1920, Anna Mitchell and Armine Gosling started a group called the Women's Franchise League. The word "franchise" means the right to vote, so you've probably guessed that the goal of the Women's Franchise League was to win voting rights for women. I joined the league and so did all the other suffragists. We held the first meeting in Anna Mitchell's living room! She lived in a beautiful brick house on Devon Row in downtown St. John's.

Anna worked hard for the suffrage movement. She knocked on a lot of doors, trying to convince people that women should have the right to vote. She was not afraid to visit powerful politicians and businessmen in their offices, even if she knew they were against women's suffrage and might get angry. Sometimes, I accompanied her on these visits. I remember that one day an influential gentleman (whom I will not mention by name, to avoid embarrassing him) became quite irritated with Anna's opinions. He told her: "Go home, madame, and learn to bake bread." This did not intimidate Anna. "I bake excellent bread" was her witty reply. Anna most certainly did not go home. She continued to knock on doors, organize meetings, write letters, and do whatever she could to fight for her right to vote. I thought she was magnificent!

> Flip back to my entry on Adeline Browning. Can you find Anna Mitchell's signature on the letter that the suffragists sent to the prime minister of Newfoundland?

> Anna worked for other worthy causes too: the Child Welfare Association and the Society for the Protection of Animals. Did you know that Anna was a vegetarian?

This is a postcard Georgina sent her uncle from Italy.

Nn *Nn*

Way back in "I," we learned that Isabella Whiteford Rogerson wrote a poem for Georgina. In 1896, the poem "To Miss Twillingate Stirling" was printed on a fancy scroll and presented to Georgina as a gift. She also received a scarf that reached all the way to the floor. The gifts were a way to thank Georgina for the many times she sang for charity. Her beautiful voice raised a lot of money, which helped a lot of people!

TO MISS TWILLINGATE STIRLING,
WITH A SCARF OF NATIVE COLORS,
PRESENTED BY REV. DR. POTTS, IN THE NAME OF
"THE WOMEN OF THE METHODIST COLLEGE AID."
A TOKEN OF ADMIRATION AND LOVE.

Oh, 'tis only a scarf. Why, it should be a crown,
   For our own "Queen of Song" is she,
And the glorious wealth of her voice of renown
   She dispenses right royally.

Aye, and loyally, too, for she loves Newfoundland,
   No matter how far she may roam;
And on earth there is nothing more touchingly grand
   Than the love of a patriot for home.

In the courts of our God we are rapt in amaze,
   Caught up by that voice into heaven,
Till entranced we can hear the bright seraphim prais
   Through the cleft air with melody riven.

Oh, this wonderful gift! for in heaven, with love,
   It survives faith and hope—aye, and prayer—
Long may Twillingate Stirling praise God up abo
   With that God-given voice, rich and rare.

The Nightingale of the North

A nightingale is a bird noted for its beautiful singing voice. It's no surprise, then, that they called Georgina Ann Stirling the Nightingale of the North. When she grew up, she became a world-famous opera singer! Georgina was born in Twillingate in 1867. She had nine brothers and sisters. What a large family! Ever since Georgina was a little girl, she loved music. It was a passion that her parents encouraged. They bought a piano, violin, and flute for all of their children to play. Soon, Georgina was performing in public. She played the church organ and she sang in concerts.

Nightingale of the North wasn't Georgina's only nickname. She also performed under the stage name Marie Toulinguet. (See her signature on the postcards above and below.)

When she was 16, Georgina moved to Toronto to study music. Later on, she went to Paris to take voice lessons. In 1890, she got her big break: she was invited to join an Italian opera house. Over the next decade, Georgina sang in famous opera houses in Europe and North America. Even the Italian royal family came out to hear her sing. Whenever she could find some free time in her busy schedule, Georgina returned to Twillingate. Everyone loved to hear her perform.

But when Georgina was in her 40s, something sad happened: she damaged her vocal chords so badly that she could no longer perform. Georgina was devastated. She decided to move in with her sisters, who were living in England. There, Georgina discovered a new interest: gardening. In 1929, she returned to Twillingate and was welcomed home with open arms by all of her neighbours and friends. She planted a beautiful garden of vegetables, flowers, and fruit trees.

Miss Georgie Stirling was the Luminary.

e has a rich full voice—a voice of eat compass; her range of notes is rprising; and she can be as clearly ard at a distance of three hundred rds as if you were very near. She cels in operatic airs, and with accompanying action. The programme the concert was:—(1) Instrumen- Duet—Vienna Gallop—Mrs. Brad- aw and ...

Evening Telegram
December 22, 1892

In 1904, a recording was made of Georgina singing in Milan, Italy. Some people believe it is the earliest known recording of a Newfoundlander!

Oo Oo

Nurse Dorothy Cherry (our entry for "C") was a NONIA nurse. I designed one of the knitting patterns that the NONIA knitters used and Elsie Holloway took these promotional photographs.

In 1934, NONIA handed over its nursing work to the government. There were no more NONIA nurses, but there were still NONIA knitters and weavers. And there still are today! About 175 knitters and weavers from across the province still work for NONIA.

Outport Nurses

Outport nurses were in short supply 100 years ago. People were getting sick in many of Newfoundland's small coastal communities, but no one was there to help them get better. A group called NONIA came to the rescue! It asked women in Newfoundland to knit sweaters and socks and then put them up for sale. The money was used to hire outport nurses. What a clever plan! NONIA stands for the Newfoundland Outport Nursing and Industrial Association. Try saying that three times fast!

Besides putting nurses in the outports, NONIA did other good work too. It paid its knitters cash. This was a big deal in the early 1900s, because most families didn't have very much money. Once, after one of the knitters received her payment, she said, "I don't know how I got home, whether on my head or on my heels. We had nothing in the house … I bought flour and other things we sorely needed." Hooray for NONIA!

Lady Elsie Allardyce (above) expanded the Outport Nursing Scheme to include the crafts production. NONIA was successful because of a three-way partnership between volunteers like Elsie, nurses like Myra Grimsley Bennett (on the right in the 1950s), and craftwomen like Beatrice Bambury (pictured below with her knitting).

Handwritten agreement between Lady Constance Harris and Nurse Myra Grimsley, September 1920.

Pp *Pp*

Evening Telegram
April 5, 1915

Nurse Parsons Goes to the Front

Miss Maisie Parsons, daughter of Mr. Edward Parsons, Chairman of the Committees of the House of Assembly, has volunteered for Red Cross work at the front, and a place has been reserved for her among the twenty places allotted to the Royal Victoria Hospital, Montreal. Nurse Parsons is employed at the General Hospital and has obtained leave. In a day or two she will leave to visit her sister, who is a patient in the Royal Victoria Hospital. Mr. Parsons has already one son in the Newfoundland Regiment.

Nurses slept in barracks or tents and worked in temporary hospitals, which were often built on the site. One example was the No. 5 Stationary Hospital, built in France in 1915 (left). This Canadian hospital moved around Europe and Africa, until it ended up in Cairo, Egypt—another place where Maysie was assigned (below).

PATIENTS ARRIVING FROM GALLIPOLI CAIRO, 1919.

Maysie Parsons

Maysie Parsons was also a nurse, although she wasn't a NONIA nurse. She studied at the General Hospital School of Nursing in St. John's. She graduated the same year that World War I broke out: 1914. Maysie knew that a lot of soldiers would need medical treatment, so she decided to enlist as a nurse with the Canadian Army Medical Corps. She was the first Newfoundland-educated nurse to join the war effort. She eventually rose through the ranks to become a lieutenant.

Lieutenant Maysie Parsons served in many places during the war, including Belgium, England, Egypt, and Greece. On June 13, 1915, Maysie wrote a letter to her father while she was stationed in La Panne, Belgium: "Tonight I am writing by the light of candle. We can't get any sleep, and have been watching the flashes of the guns, etc., all along the lines for hours. It really seems that the fighting is all around us. I am glad I came but it certainly seems strange."

Two kinds of nurses served in World War I. Professional nurses, like Maysie (shown here in her dress uniform), were formally trained at a nursing school. There were also volunteer nurses, who only received several weeks of training—like my sister, Janet.

When Maysie wrote that letter to her father, she was nursing at L'Hôpital de l'Océan in La Panne, Belgium. It was a seaside hotel that was turned into a 100-bed field hospital.

Maysie received four medals for her service: the Royal Red Cross, the 1914–1915 Star, the Military Medal from King George V, and the Allied Victory Medal.

Explorer William Cormack met Ann in 1822 while he was trekking across Newfoundland. He described her in his diary as a community leader: "She is indefatigably industrious and useful, and immediately or remotely related to, or connected with, the whole population of the bay, over whom she commands a remarkable degree of maternal influence and respect."

Qq *Qq*

The *Benjamin Franklin* was a formidable enemy. It had eight large guns and a crew of 120 sailors: more than a match for the tiny *Industry*.

The Queen of St. George's Bay

They say you shouldn't mix business with pleasure, but what about mixing business with adventure? That's what Ann Hulan did. The year was 1812 and America was at war with Britain. As a British colony, Newfoundland was swept up in the war, too. The greatest threat was at sea. American privateers prowled the ocean, looking for British ships to capture and bring to American ports. (A privateer was a person or ship that the government authorized to seize enemy vessels.)

On August 7, an American privateer called the *Benjamin Franklin* captured Ann Hulan's schooner, the *Industry*. Ann was taken prisoner along with her three-person crew. They had been sailing from Ann's home in St. George's Bay to St. John's to sell 152 barrels of cured salmon. Ann owned the schooner as well as 71 barrels of salmon, so she had a lot to lose if the Americans seized the ship and its cargo.

The *Benjamin Franklin* took Ann and her crew to New York as prisoners of war. In September, a Marine Court of Inquiry heard their case. Ann testified that the *Industry* was her vessel and that it was not a threat to the United States—it was a small schooner she used to send her fish to market. Ann was a persuasive speaker. Her testimony convinced the authorities that she and her crew should be set free and that the *Industry* and its cargo of salmon should be returned to her. Ann and her crew were back in St. George's Bay in time for Christmas.

I think Ann named her vessel the *Industry* because she was such an industrious woman. In the late 1700s, she and her husband, John, established a farm and fish exporting business in St. George's Bay. After John died in the early 1800s, Ann took over and expanded the business. She raised cows and opened a dairy; she experimented with new varieties of potatoes; and every year she exported hundreds of barrels of cured salmon to international markets (at her own risk, as we have learned!). As her enterprise grew, it became an economic pillar of the community. Soon, Ann Hulan became known as the Queen of St. George's Bay. All hail Queen Ann!

Rr Rr

Girl Guides have been meeting in Newfoundland and Labrador for more than a century. The first company formed in 1912 and its members camped at Lawrence Pond, Conception Bay. The movement steadily grew over the coming years. By 1923, there were 250 Girl Guides in Newfoundland and Labrador. That same year, Lady Elsie Allardyce (we met her on page 31) made the dominion's Guides official members of the Girl Guides Association in Britain. After Confederation in 1949, the Girl Guides of Newfoundland and Labrador left the British association and joined the Girl Guides of Canada.

Dora Oake Russell

Dora Oake Russell was born on Change Islands in 1912. When she was older, she moved to St. John's and became a teacher at the St. Mary's Church of England School. She was passionate about education and recognized the important role that teachers play in our society. When the government proposed cutting teacher salaries in 1932, Dora objected in a letter to the *Evening Telegram*. She wrote that the move would be "a discredit to the government, and a drastic violation of all the rules of honour and fair play."

In 1945, Dora Russell began a new job: she became the *Evening Telegram*'s first Woman's Editor. It was an important job. The *Evening Telegram* was one of the largest newspapers in Newfoundland and Labrador and a lot of people read it. Dora Russell was a remarkable woman who did a remarkable job. She reported on politics, wrote fiction, and, perhaps most impressive of all, created a new feature for the newspaper called *Woman of the Week*. Every Saturday, Dora profiled a different notable woman for the newspaper. Her readers loved it! Russell profiled 140 women for the *Telegram* during her time as editor. Her work also inspired other women to become reporters—including Grace Sparkes, Cassie Brown, and Sylvia Wigh.

But Russell's interests roamed far beyond writing. She was also a teacher, a Girl Guide leader, and an astronomer. She knew a lot about stars and the night sky and she helped to found the St. John's Centre Branch of the Royal Astronomical Society. Dora also helped a lot of Girl Guides get their astronomy badges. I wonder what her favourite constellation was?

Dora worked for the *Evening Telegram* in this building. Elsie Holloway (our entry for "E") was a Woman of the Week in 1946!

A recurring topic in Dora's newspaper columns was the need for more women to become politicians. "You'll see Newfoundland come out of the fog when she has more women involved in politics," she once wrote. "I'm all for any woman who has the nerve to take it on."

The first four students of the School of Nursing—Elizabeth Redmond, Madge Cullian, Elizabeth Blackmore, and Jessie Swyers—standing for morning inspection in the Crowdy Ward.

Ss Ss

Mary Southcott

In 1914, Maysie Parsons (we met Maysie back at "P") graduated from the General Hospital School of Nursing in St. John's. Well, the person who founded that school was Mary Southcott. Mary was born in St. John's, but in order to become a nurse, she had to study in London, England. At that time, there were no nursing schools in Newfoundland and Labrador. Mary Southcott thought that people shouldn't have to travel far away to become nurses, so she decided to establish a school in St. John's. She joined forces with the General Hospital to open a School of Nursing in 1903. It was suddenly a lot easier for people from Newfoundland and Labrador to become nurses!

But Mary Southcott didn't stop there. She also saw a great need to improve the health care services that were available to pregnant women, babies, and children. She created training programs for midwives and opened a maternity hospital in downtown St. John's. Mothers and children were healthier because of Mary Southcott's hard work! But health care wasn't her only passion. Mary Southcott was also active in the suffrage movement and she was a member of the Current Events Club, just like her friends Fannie McNeil, Armine Gosling, and me!

Mary Southcott also had a deep interest in botany. In 1915, she published a book called *Some Newfoundland Wild Flowers*. I wonder how she found the time to do everything! The photographs below show her gardening at Waterford Hall, a military convalescent hospital she ran. The photograph on the left was taken in the General Hospital yard.

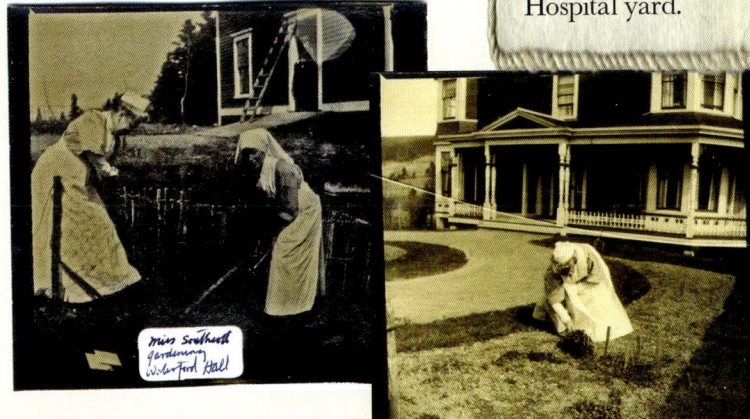

Site of Mary Travers's tavern in 1833

Mary's tavern was on the corner of King's Road and Duckworth Street.

Mary Travers

Mary Travers was a tavern owner who stood up for what she believed was right. The year was 1833. Newfoundland had just put its very first elected government in office. The government was so new that its members didn't yet have a building where they could meet. They asked Mary Travers if they could use her tavern, and she said yes. Over the next five months, the government members met almost every single day in her tavern. The politicians made all sorts of important decisions and they passed all sorts of important laws. But they also forgot something very important. They forgot to pay Mary Travers the rent they owed her for the use of her tavern! Even worse, they tried to get out of paying her altogether. They said that because Newfoundland was still a British colony, Britain should pay the rent instead of the Newfoundland government.

Mary Travers knew they were wrong and she was not intimidated. She went to court and a judge ordered the Newfoundland government to stop using the tavern. He also gave Mary Travers permission to seize some of the government's property until the rent was paid. She took possession of some books and desks, and she also seized the fancy chair, hat, and mace that belonged to the Speaker of the House of Assembly. (A mace is a special staff that represents the government's authority.) Three cheers for Mary Travers!

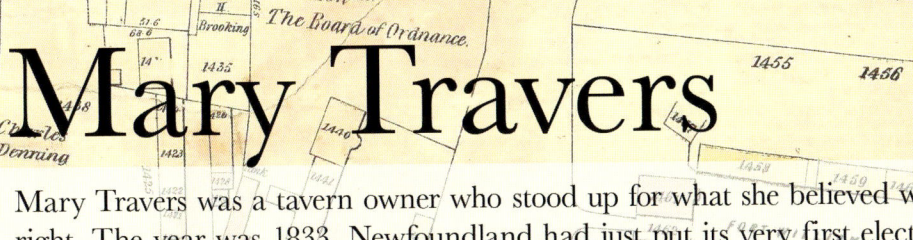

The government owed Mary Travers for five months' rent plus coal, wood, candles, and servants: a total of 193 pounds, 19 shillings, and 12 pence. That's over $35,000 in today's money!

Some of the items Mary seized from the government were eventually put up for auction. A gentleman named Mr. Leary bought them, but he didn't keep them for long—everything was eventually returned to the government, including the mace, pictured above, which was used until Newfoundland and Labrador joined Canada in 1949.

41

Uu *Uu*

Lobbyists are groups that try to influence politicians to change the rules that govern our society. This image shows members of the WCTU passing out pamphlets to Newfoundland politicians on the steps of the Colonial Building.

Isabella Whiteford Rogerson and Anna Mitchell were both members of the WCTU—they were also my entries for the letters "I" and "M"!

Union (the WCTU)

The Women's Franchise League was not the first group that fought for women's voting rights in Newfoundland. Decades earlier, there was a Union—the Women's Christian Temperance Union (or WCTU for short). It formed in 1890 and its leaders were some of the most influential and intelligent women in Newfoundland—like Emma Peters and Lady Jeanette Thorburn. Both were skilled public speakers who were already well-known and well-respected members of society. Jessie Ohman, a talented writer who worked as a journalist and a poet, was also involved.

LADY THORBURN.

All three women had strong opinions and they were not shy about sharing their thoughts with the public. One of their strongest opinions was that women should be allowed to vote. They, along with the other members of the WCTU, fought long and hard for this goal. They wrote letters to the government and to newspapers, and they published magazines, organized marches, signed petitions, and gave speeches. They accomplished so much by working together ... But they were too far ahead of their time. In 1893, the government of the day refused to give women the right to vote. Sometimes things don't work out the way they should. That doesn't mean there is no hope. The trailblazing women of the WCTU inspired the next generation of suffragists, which included people like Armine Gosling, Fannie McNeil, and me: Agnes Ayre!

MRS. OHMAN,
GRAND SUPT. OF JUV. TEMPLES, I.O.G.T.

MRS. PETERS.

The WCTU was an international organization. It formed in Ohio in 1874 and by 1890 had spread to other parts of the world, including Canada, Australia, New Zealand, and Newfoundland.

Amelia Earhart

Amelia Earhart was an aviator from Kansas. She made two historic flights from Newfoundland. The first was on June 17, 1928. Amelia was a passenger on board the airplane *Friendship*. It took off from Trepassey on June 17 and landed in the United Kingdom 20 hours and 40 minutes later. That flight made Amelia the first woman to cross the Atlantic Ocean by air. Four years later, Amelia was once again in Newfoundland. This time she wasn't a passenger, though: she was the pilot. On May 20, 1932, Amelia Earhart took off from Harbour Grace in her bright red Lockheed Vega 5B. She landed in Northern Ireland 14 hours and 56 minutes later. She had completed the very first solo transatlantic flight made by a woman. Hip hip hooray!

Venturesome Visitors

Over the years, many Venturesome Visitors have come to Newfoundland and Labrador. Here are two.

Mina Benson Hubbard

Mina Benson Hubbard was an explorer. In 1905, she left her home in New York to trek across Labrador's unmapped interior. She led an expedition that walked from North West River to Ungava Bay. Two years earlier, Mina's husband, Leonidas Hubbard, died while trying to travel across the same route. Mina decided to finish her husband's work. She knew it was a dangerous journey, but she was determined. Her strength and resolve paid off. After two months of backpacking, paddling, and camping, Mina led her expedition into Ungava Bay on August 27, 1905. Success! She also produced the first maps of the Naskaupi and George river systems—and they were accurate enough to be accepted by the American and British Geographical Societies.

Three other people joined Mina on her amazing journey: George Elson (paddling in the front of the canoe), Joe Iserhoffe (sitting behind George), Job Chapies (standing in the second canoe), and Gilbert Blake (the man on the top right). Remember Lydia Campbell (my entry for "L")? Gilbert was her grandson!

THE WATER LILY.

Vol. I.   JANUARY, 1892.   No. 1.

Beggar.—Would you please give me a few cents, sir?

Sir W. Whiteway.—Where is your husband, can't he support you and your children?

Beggar.—He has been drinking those six months and earned nothing.

Sir W.—Why don't you keep him at home?

Beggar.—I can't sir. The only way I can stop him drinking is to try and close up the liquor stores. While they're open he'll drink.

Sir W.—Ah! You are one of those for whom the ladies ask a vote?

Beggar—Yes, sir, bless them.

Sir W.—(Turning abruptly away). Then I shall give you neither vote nor money.

Do you remember our entry for the letter "U"? (Pssst: it was the Women's Christian Temperance Union.) The WCTU was the earliest known group in Newfoundland to fight for women's right to vote. Well, the WCTU had a magazine, which it called *The Water Lily*. Jessie Ohman, who was a member of the WCTU, was also the editor of *The Water Lily*. The magazine published all sorts of articles and cartoons that promoted women's suffrage. When the government refused to give voting rights to women in 1893, *The Water Lily* was not shy about voicing its displeasure. Jessie Ohman wrote: "A legislature composed of such narrow-minded men must be ousted." *The Water Lily* helped to spread the word about women's suffrage across Newfoundland. It also inspired young women and girls to become suffragists when they grew up.

The Water Lily is thought to be the first women's magazine published in Newfoundland. It did not last long, only two years. Jessie Murray Ohman and her husband, Nils, a Swedish watchmaker, emigrated to Montreal some time after the last issue in 1893.

Sir William Whiteway was the prime minister in Jessie's day. By the time I was a suffragist in the 1920s, Sir Richard Squires was prime minister, and he was just as opposed to suffrage as Whiteway was.

Xx *Xx*

NEWFOUNDLAND
General Election: Oct. 29, 1928
St. John's East

| 1 | ALDERDICE, Frederick (United Newfoundland Party) | X |

NEWFOUNDLAND
General Election: Oct. 29, 1928
Harbour Grace

| 1 | ARCHIBALD, Frank C. (Liberal Party) | X |
| 2 | BENNETT, John R. (United Newfoundland Party) | |

NEWFOUNDLAND
By-Election 1930
Lewisporte

| 1 | SQUIRES, Helena E. (Liberal) | X |

Remember Prime Minister Richard Squires—the man we wrote to in 1920? In 1930 his wife, Lady Helena Squires, became the first woman elected to the House of Assembly.

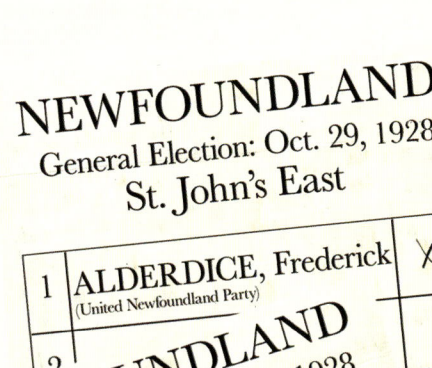

This is a photograph of some of the members of the Women's Franchise League. We were so happy when all of our work paid off! Do you recognize any of these faces? I'm there, sitting on the left. To the right of me is my sister, Janet. And standing second from the left in the back row is the fabulous Fannie McNeil!

When Anna Barnes Mitchell finally marked her X in 1928, she had been fighting for the vote for almost 40 years!

X marks the spot

X marks the spot on pirate maps. It also marks the spot on voting ballots! I have introduced you to many suffragists in this book. Now it's time for good news: our years of hard work ended in success in 1925! After gathering thousands and thousands of signatures on petitions, after writing countless letters to the government and to newspapers, after publishing magazines, after visiting door to door to drum up support, and after marching through the streets of St. John's, we were finally victorious on March 9, 1925. On that day, the Newfoundland government passed a bill granting women the right to vote. It became law on April 13. Hooray Armine Gosling! Hooray Fannie McNeil! And hooray to so many others: Adeline Browning, Anna Mitchell, Mary Southcott, Jessie Ohman, and to all the eXcellent women who made their society a better place!

Women cast ballots in their first general election on October 29, 1928. They had a 90 per cent voter turnout—which means that most women marked big beautiful Xs on their ballots that day! Can anyone play "For She's a Jolly Good Fellow" on the Xylophone?

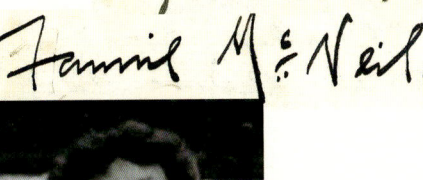

Margaret Duley

Elsie Holloway

Mary Southcott

Jessie Ohman

It was a different story in Labrador. No one there (woman or man) had the right to vote until 1946.

Yes to the Vote!

By working together, women won the right to vote. In Newfoundland, we came together under the Women's Franchise League. But we were part of a larger, international network of suffragists, too. In the late 1800s and early 1900s, women from many countries were fighting for the right to vote. We noticed that by talking to each other, we could learn from each other. We joined the International Women's Suffrage Alliance (IWSA). It had formed in Washington in 1902. By the 1920s, its membership included representatives from 46 countries.

IWSA members stayed in touch mostly by mail and through the pages of the alliance's newspaper, *Jus Suffragii*. Sometimes, though, IWSA members met in person at conventions. It was an excellent opportunity to talk with like-minded women from around the world. In 1923, my friend May Kennedy represented Newfoundland at the convention in Rome, Italy. That was the year Newfoundland suffragists officially joined the IWSA. Egypt, India, Japan, Palestine, Romania, and Spain also joined that year. In 1926, May Kennedy went to a second convention in Paris—this time she was joined by my other good friend, Adeline Browning.

By then, as you know, Newfoundland women had already won the right to vote. But there still was plenty of work to do! Women did not have the same economic rights as men, and the IWSA focused its attention on this. It also fought for suffrage in countries where women still did not have voting rights (in France, for example, women didn't win the right to vote until 1944!). Because of its expanded role, the alliance changed its name to the International Alliance of Women for Suffrage and Equal Citizenship.

Mary (May) Kennedy was the treasurer of the Women's Franchise League. This is her signature on the letter that we wrote to the prime minister in 1920. She even ran for St. John's city council once, along with Fannie McNeil. Too bad they didn't win!

Australia 1902

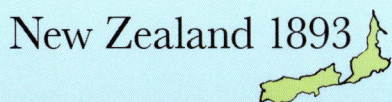

New Zealand 1893

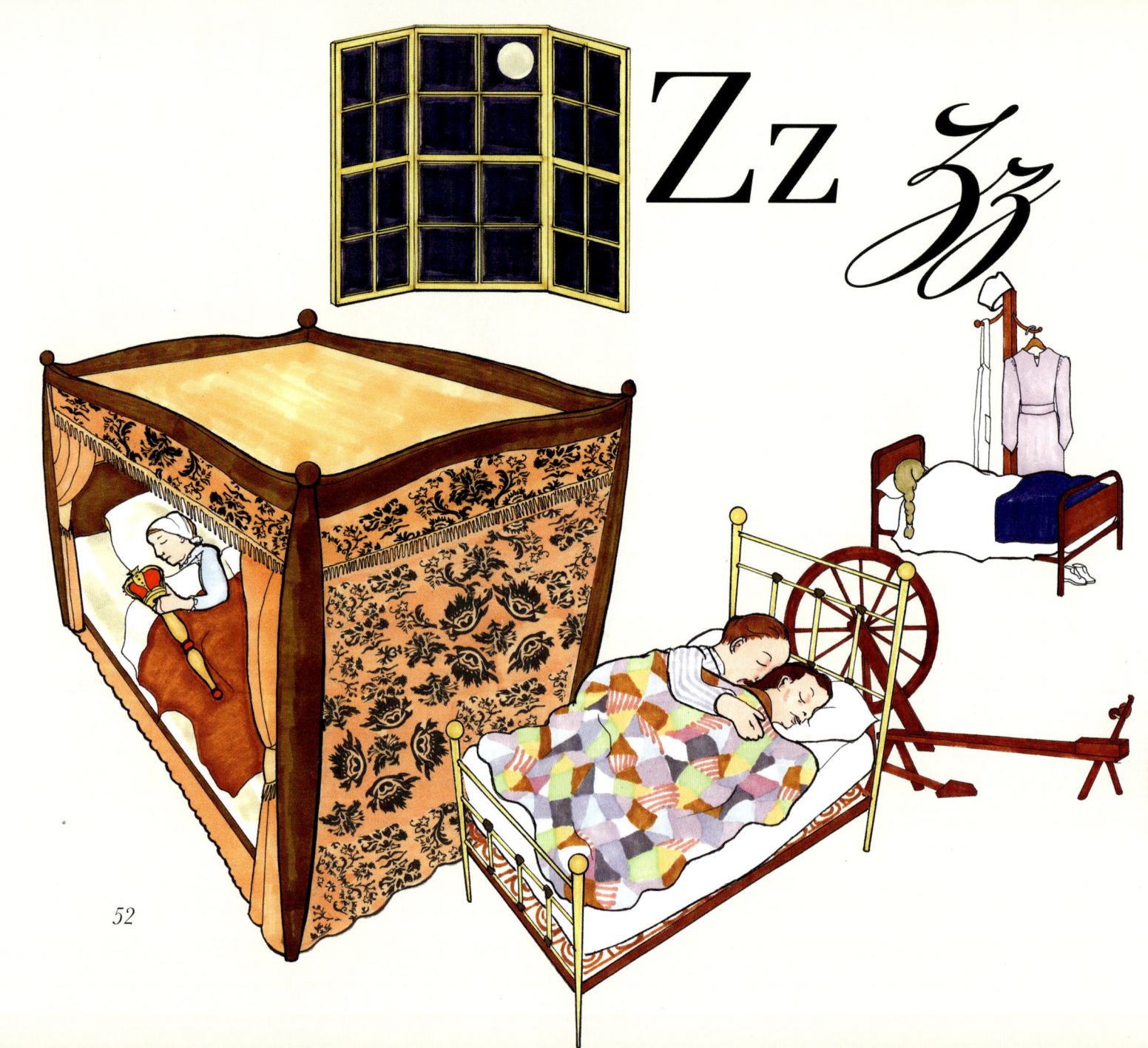

Zzzzzzzzz

I think all of those busy women must be getting sleepy after accomplishing so much. I'm getting tired just thinking about it!

Which brings us to:

Zzzzzzzzzzzzzzzzzzzzzz…………

(But remember that tomorrow is another day!)

Aa Bb Cc Dd Ee Ff Gg Hh Ii Jj Kk Ll Mm Nn Oo Pp Qq Rr Ss Tt Uu Vv Ww Xx Yy Zz

The Suffragist's Pledge

This is my book, and I pledge to do all in my power to promote and preserve the right of all citizens to vote in my nation.

_____

(Your signature here.)

Image sources and page of appearance: A.C. Hunter Library 5, 8, 9, 15, 18, 19, 26, 28; Archives and Special Collections, Memorial University 2, 3, 5, 6, 11, 12, 15, 20, 21, 22, 25, 26, 27, 29, 30, 31, 39, 45, 47, 48, 49; *Book of Newfoundland* (retrieved using the Digital Archives Initiative [DAI]) 12; *Canadian Guiding Badges and Insignia Resource published by the Girl Guides of Canada- Guides du Canada, Ontario Council Archives, 2009* 36; City of St. John's Archives 18, 40, 41; Clerk of the House of Assembly of Newfoundland and Labrador 41; *Distaff* (DAI) 4, 5, 15, 33, 49; Elizabeth Miller and Kelly Russell 37; Evelyn Peyton Murphy 28, 29; *Evening Telegram* 7, 13, 29, 32; Greenspond Historical Society 20; Library of Congress Prints and Photographs Division (LC-DIG-ppmsca-31771) 44; Margot Duley 9, 49; Maritime History Archive 10, 11, 50; *Newfoundland Quarterly* (DAI) 15, 27, 30, 49; Queen's University Web Archives 32; The Rooms Provincial Archives Division 4, 6, 7, 10, 11, 12, 13, 20, 48, 49; The Rooms Provincial Art Gallery 22, 23; Rosina Holwell 22, 23; *Royal Reader Book I* (DAI) 35; *Them Days* 24; *The Water Lily* (DAI) 43, 46, 47.

We also want to thank: Sandra Barnes and the staff of the Clerk of the House of Assembly; Mina Campbell; Margot Duley; Rosina Holwell; Elizabeth Miller and Kelly Russell; Evelyn Peyton Murphy; Suzanne Sexty; Margot Walsh, Provincial Commissioner Girl Guides of Canada; Linda White; the staff at Archives and Special Collections and the Centre for Newfoundland Studies, QEII Library; the staff at the Maritime History Archive; the staff at the Newfoundland Collection, A.C. Hunter Library; and the staff at The Rooms.